In memory of

Martin F. Buell, MD

And his wife,

Mary L. Buell

CR

Somerset County Library System
100 Collins Street
Crisfield, MD 21817
CRISFIELD BRANCH

OUR EXTREME EARTH

EARTHQUAKES

REBECCA FELIX

Consulting Editor, Diane Craig, M.A./Reading Specialist

Sandcastle

An Imprint of Abdo Publishing
abdopublishing.com

abdopublishing.com

Published by Abdo Publishing, a division of ABDO, PO Box 398166, Minneapolis, Minnesota 55439. Copyright © 2018 by Abdo Consulting Group, Inc. International copyrights reserved in all countries. No part of this book may be reproduced in any form without written permission from the publisher. SandCastle™ is a trademark and logo of Abdo Publishing.

Printed in the United States of America, North Mankato, Minnesota

102017
012018

THIS BOOK CONTAINS RECYCLED MATERIALS

Design: Kelly Doudna, Mighty Media, Inc.
Production: Mighty Media, Inc.
Editor: Liz Salzmann
Cover Photographs: iStockphoto, Shutterstock
Interior Photographs: Courtesy of the Archives, California Institute of Technology; iStockphoto; Shutterstock

Publisher's Cataloging-in-Publication Data

Names: Felix, Rebecca, author.
Title: Earthquakes / by Rebecca Felix.
Description: Minneapolis, Minnesota : Abdo Publishing, 2018. | Series: Our extreme earth |
Identifiers: LCCN 2017946707 | ISBN 9781532112225 (lib.bdg.) |
    ISBN 9781614799641 (ebook)
Subjects: LCSH: Seismology--Juvenile literature. | Earthquakes--Juvenile literature. |
    Earth sciences--Juvenile literature.
Classification: DDC 551.22--dc23
LC record available at https://lccn.loc.gov/2017946707

SandCastle™ Level: Fluent

SandCastle™ books are created by a team of professional educators, reading specialists, and content developers around five essential components—phonemic awareness, phonics, vocabulary, text comprehension, and fluency—to assist young readers as they develop reading skills and strategies and increase their general knowledge. All books are written, reviewed, and leveled for guided reading, early reading intervention, and Accelerated Reader® programs for use in shared, guided, and independent reading and writing activities to support a balanced approach to literacy instruction. The SandCastle™ series has four levels that correspond to early literacy development. The levels are provided to help teachers and parents select appropriate books for young readers.

EMERGING • BEGINNING • TRANSITIONAL • FLUENT

CONTENTS

About Earthquakes	4
Think About It	22
Glossary	24

ABOUT EARTHQUAKES

An earthquake is when the earth shakes. **Cracks** can form.

The ground moves.
It may rise or fall.

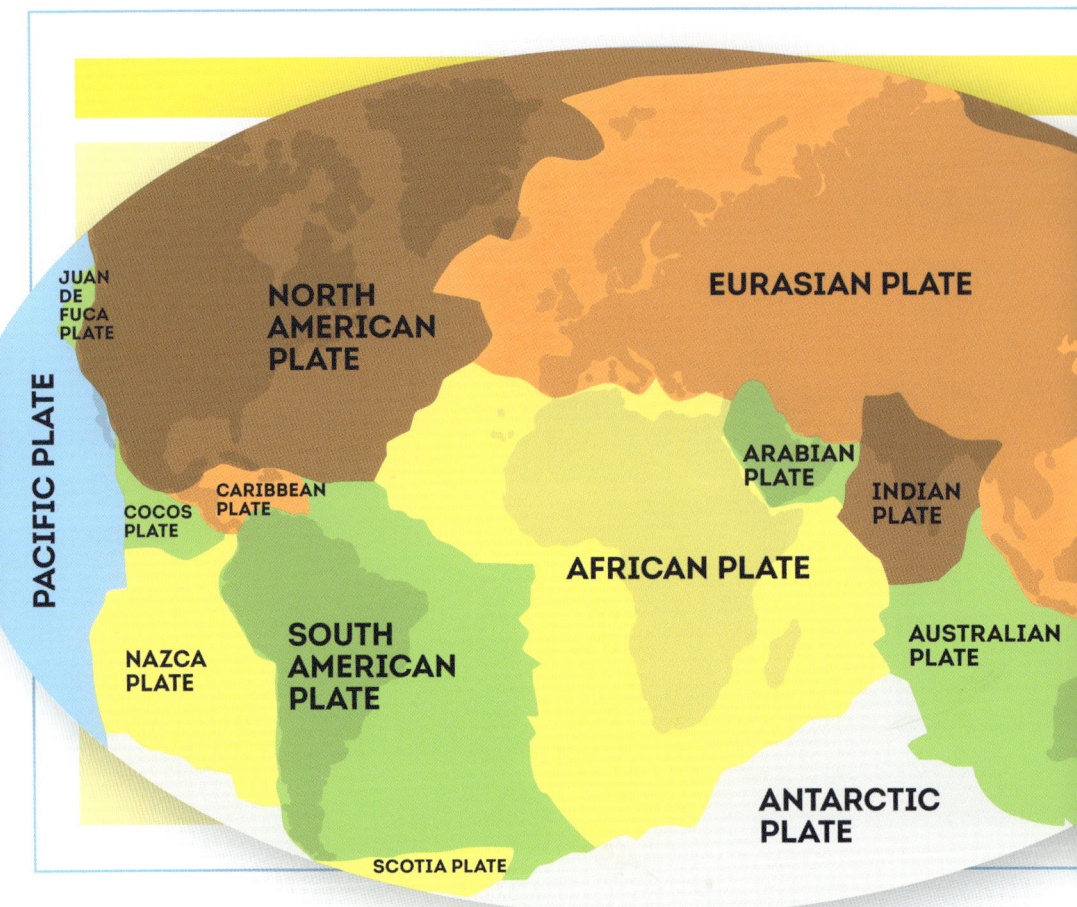

Large plates make up the earth's surface. The plates fit together.

Faults form where plates meet.

Earth's plates move. They can slide **sideways**. This can cause **faults**.

Or they may push against each other. One edge rises over the other.

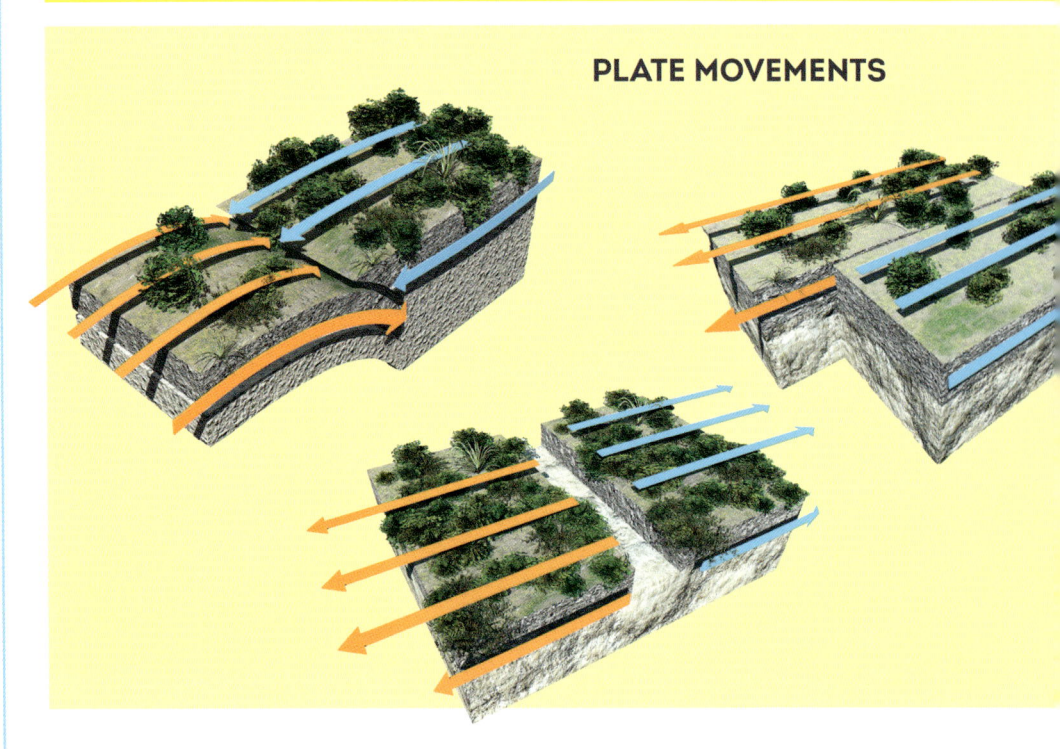

The plates can also break.
The pieces move apart.

All of these movements can cause quakes.

Quakes occur all over the world.

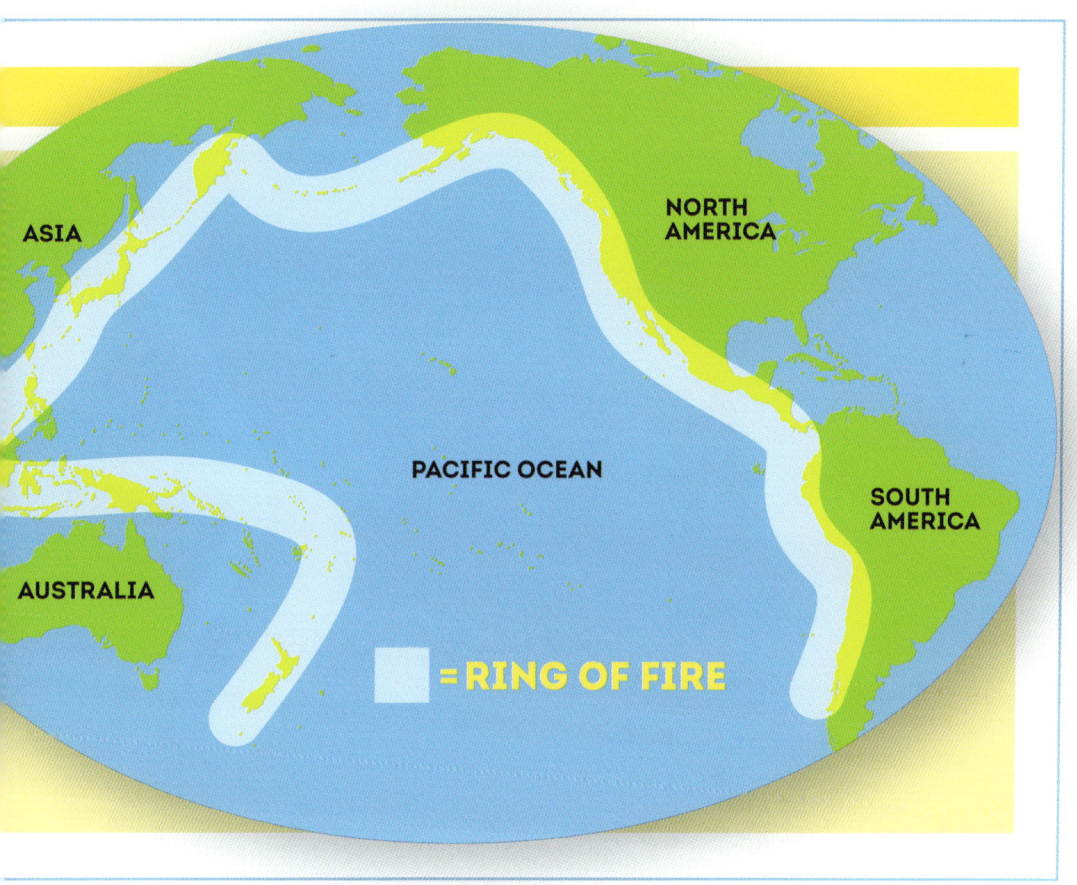

Many happen in the Ring of Fire.
This is in the Pacific Ocean.

Quakes on the ocean floor cannot be felt by people.

But strong ones can create **tsunamis**.

Strong quakes can happen on land too.

They cause **landslides**. Buildings fall down.

Charles Francis Richter was a **seismologist**. He studied quakes.

He created a quake scale.
It measures quake strength.

People prepare for quakes. They build **structures** that can survive quakes.

People also gather supplies they might need. This can save lives.

THINK ABOUT IT

Have you been in an earthquake? What did you do to stay safe?

GLOSSARY

crack – a narrow hole or opening.

fault – a crack in the earth's crust along which movement occurs.

landslide – when a large amount of rocks or dirt slides down a hill.

seismologist – a scientist who studies earthquakes.

sideways – to or from the side.

structure – something that has been built, such as a building or a bridge.

tsunami – a group of powerful ocean waves that can destroy areas.